THE ETA COHEN
VIOLIN METHOD
BOOK ONE

THE ETA COHEN VIOLIN METHOD
BOOK ONE
Sixth Edition

Sixth edition edited by
Maureen Smith

(Daughter of Eta Cohen and
Professor of Violin at The Royal
Academy of Music, London)

NOVELLO

part of The **Music Sales** *Group of Companies*

London / New York / Paris / Sydney / Copenhagen / Berlin / Madrid / Hong Kong / Tokyo

Published by
Novello Publishing Limited,
14-15 Berners Street, London W1T 3LJ, UK.

Exclusive Distributors:
Music Sales Limited
Distribution Centre, Newmarket Road, Bury St Edmunds, Suffolk IP33 3YB, UK.
Music Sales Corporation
257 Park Avenue South, New York, NY 10010, USA.
Music Sales Pty Limited
20 Resolution Drive, Caringbah, NSW 2229, Australia.

Order No. NOV140019
ISBN: 978-1-84938-774-3
This book © Copyright 2012 by Novello Publishing

Design by Fresh Lemon
Photography by Matthew Ward
Models: Lucy Anderson, Rhianna Bryant and Jaden Stauch

Back cover photograph of Eta Cohen by Denis Thorpe,
© Copyright Guardian News & Media Ltd 2012.

CD recorded, mixed and mastered by Jonas Persson
Backing tracks by Rick Cardinali

All tracks © Dorsey Brothers Music Limited

Recordings produced by Maureen Smith
Violin: Alexandra Wood

Printed in the EU

INTRODUCTION

Our mother, Eta Cohen, now retired and in her mid 90s, was a charismatic and progressive teacher whose violin method was a pioneering project. The book speaks for itself, and one of Eta's great strengths has proved to be her ability to communicate with those she has never met. However, as violinists ourselves we would like to convey here a little of our first-hand knowledge of Eta's unique teaching philosophy and innovative methods.

Eta first started to teach when she was only 17. She looked for a violin tutor to assist her, but in 1933 there were no such books on the market. Undeterred, Eta painstakingly wrote out each lesson for her students by hand. She based the lessons on familiar tunes and organised the material so that the process of learning was both entertaining and systematic. These lessons became the foundation for her method, which was subsequently published as a book. The tutor was an immediate success and was followed by a number of sequels.

Her great insight was that teaching the violin would be most successful if approached incrementally. She often told the story of her first violin lesson: the teacher said, 'here's the violin, here's the bow, now play'. As a rebuttal to this 'deep-end' approach to learning which left the pupil stranded and overwhelmed, she taught only one new idea at a time, whether it be a key, a rhythm or a technique. She believed that a slow start based on good style, intonation and sound resulted in much faster progress in the end, and also avoided the acquisition of bad habits. Consequently, the order of the exercises was carefully considered. For instance, rather than encouraging beginners to play on all strings at once, Eta advocated focusing on the D and A strings only. This made it easier for pupils to tune their violins, produce a good sound, and sing and pluck melodies within one octave. The finger pattern in D Major – the first key they learnt – also had the advantage of being the same for both strings.

The careful organisation of the method meant that it was a great equalizer because any child could make good progress almost irrespective of talent. Eta also questioned the widely-held belief that unfettered enjoyment and the maintenance of high standards must be incompatible. She believed that playing well brings intense satisfaction whereas playing badly results only in frustration, and that the secret was to make the material so attractive to pupils that it was irresistible. To this end, each technical point was consolidated not only through an accompanying exercise, but also through a selection of mouth-watering pieces.

The rigour of Eta's method was matched only by her personal teaching skills, which were fuelled by her love of children. She had energy, patience and imagination, tailoring her method to each pupil, and treating parents and pupils as friends. She believed that at least one parent should be present at lessons and supervise practice at home, and that conditions for learning should be made as alluring as possible. She would even check that the lesson time didn't coincide with a favourite TV programme. She divided each lesson into a variety of technical and musical challenges to maintain interest and concentration, and wrote down a program of work each week in the pupil's notebook. She also understood the pull of incentives: many of these were built into her method, but she also gave small rewards.

Eta's pupils now occupy many prominent positions in the musical profession. They lead orchestras, play in chamber groups or are musical managers. Some of them have children of their own who have also learnt the violin from Eta's books. We hope that this new edition will make Eta's method available to yet another generation of aspiring violinists who cannot experience her first-hand as a teacher, but can benefit from her continuing wisdom and advice.

Maureen and Hazel Smith, 2012.

ETA'S FOREWORD

This Method can be used for private or class tuition with children of all ages, as well as adult beginners. I would give the following advice to teachers as the most effective way of using this book.

Rate of progress

Teach one point at a time and do not move forward until each stage has been thoroughly assimilated and understood. Remember that if pupils move very slowly at the beginning they will always make more rapid progress at the next stage.

The book is divided into 30 'steps'. There is no inflexible rule about the speed at which pupils should progress – it will vary according to ability and size of class; remember quality is more important than speed. Each step may take anything from one to four weeks (or even longer) to complete, and previous steps can be revised; it is inadvisable to cover more than one step per lesson: every step introduces something new and it is always best to allow time for the proper absorption of the new work or ideas.

Which string?

It is best to start with one string – the D string – and then use only D and A for some time. Good tone is easier to achieve on these two strings and difficulties of tuning and reading are minimised. Encourage pupils to sing the music (easiest within the compass of D–D'). I have never experienced any reading difficulties with pupils taught this way.

Bowing

After the first few lessons introduce the bow-hold *(Step 6)* and then attempt easy bowing exercises. Proceed very gradually, first practising away from the violin *(see photographs 20 & 21)*, then on the D string using only the top half of the bow (middle to point), and then on the A string but always keeping the bow moving at the same speed. Next, teach bowing from the heel to middle of the bow and finally join the two half bows into whole bows *(Step 14)*.

For some time use only half or whole bows, with a constant bow speed. This way the pupil can concentrate on using the full bow without worrying about the different lengths or speeds of bow. They can also listen more easily to the pitch without other distraction, and if they play slowly enough, can immediately adjust any note which is slightly out of tune.

Only when the pupil is accustomed to using every inch of the hair should they go on to play with various lengths and speeds of bow.

There are many bowing marks through the book, so that if a pupil stops in the middle of a piece they can carry on using the correct up or down bow without having to go back to the beginning of a bar or line. They should always be encouraged to pick up their place immediately at any point in the music indicated by the teacher.

Dynamics

It is difficult to know when to introduce dynamics. From the beginning encourage pupils to play with a firm, strong tone with the bow near the bridge. Later, show them how to play softly, away from the bridge, and gradually introduce various shades of tone in between.

Try introducing some tonal variety from Step 19 onwards, but it may be some time before pupils can accomplish this successfully. The main objective should be to achieve a good sound through correct bowing technique and training pupils to listen for tone quality as well as for correct intonation.

ETA COHEN

CONTENTS

PARTS OF THE VIOLIN

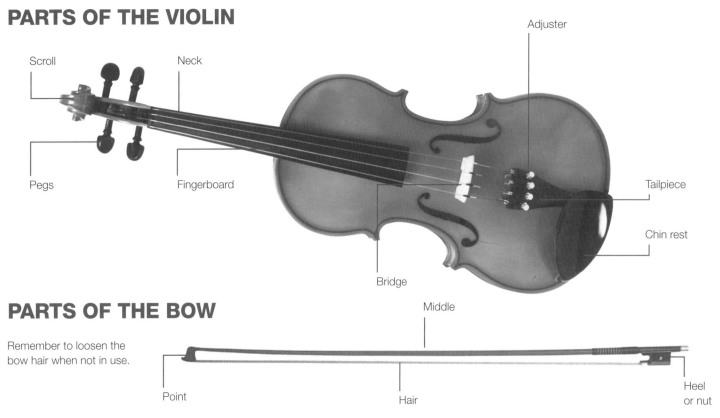

Scroll

Neck

Adjuster

Pegs

Fingerboard

Tailpiece

Chin rest

Bridge

Middle

PARTS OF THE BOW

Remember to loosen the bow hair when not in use.

Point

Hair

Heel or nut

TUNING

You will only use the D string at first, so tune it at the beginning of each practice. Keep checking to see if it needs retuning.

A Hold the violin upright on your knee, left hand around the neck, left thumb free for plucking *(photograph 1)*.

B Keep perfect silence and listen to the note D being played. (When practising at home ask someone else to play the note on the piano, or use a tuning fork, or an iPhone app.)

C After D has been played a second time, hum the note.

D After a moment's pause, hum it again, to see if you can remember the sound. Be sure that you have the exact pitch in your head.

E If you use an adjuster pluck the D string with the left thumb and turn the adjuster with the right hand *(photograph 1)*. At the same time, listen carefully, while the teacher continues to play the note. If you use the peg for tuning, turn it very slowly with the left hand, and pluck with the right thumb – turn the peg away from you if the string is flat and towards you if it is sharp. Press the peg firmly into the hole all the time while continuing to pluck the string with the right thumb until the string sounds in tune *(photograph 2)*.

Tuning with adjusters
Turn adjuster with right hand.
Pluck string with left thumb.

Tuning with pegs
Turn peg with left hand.
Pluck string with right thumb.

BANJO POSITION FOR RHYTHM EXERCISES

3

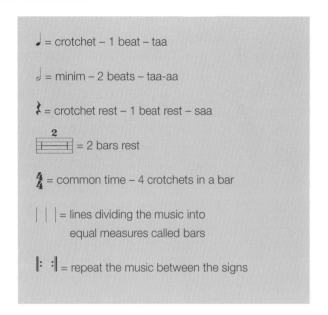

♩ = crotchet – 1 beat – taa

♩ = minim – 2 beats – taa-aa

𝄽 = crotchet rest – 1 beat rest – saa

𝄾 = 2 bars rest

4/4 = common time – 4 crotchets in a bar

| | | = lines dividing the music into
equal measures called bars

𝄆 : 𝄇 = repeat the music between the signs

Violin tucked under right arm, scroll sloping upwards, right fingers under fingerboard and right thumb free for plucking.

RHYTHM EXERCISES ON 'D' STRING PLAYED PIZZICATO

Plucked

1 Say the rhythm names **2** Clap the time **3** Play in banjo position

CD 1 & 3

When playing a minim pizzicato, you cannot hold the note for 2 beats so just think of it as a long note.

BANJO POSITION FOR FINGER EXERCISES
Sit or Stand

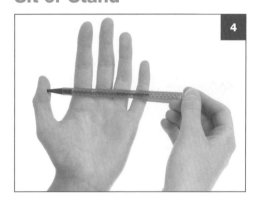

Hold your left hand up and place a pencil across the third crease of your 1st finger and fleshy part of your thumb to form a V. Your thumb should be relaxed – not stiff or bent.

Place the violin (instead of the pencil) with the third crease of your 1st finger against the top edge of the fingerboard. Violin against the fleshy part of your thumb. Thumb opposite your 1st finger.

Place the violin under your right arm and push your left elbow forward. This brings your thumb more underneath and fingers over the strings. Then place your fingers firmly on the D string, stand them up squarely, 1st and 2nd fingers apart, 2nd and 3rd close together.

This shows the V formed by the thumb and 1st finger. Notice the straight line from the knuckles towards the elbow.

This is your banjo position. Lift your fingers off the D string and you will be ready to play. Be sure to keep a straight line from your knuckles to your elbows.

Practise this position every day until you can hold the violin with ease – you will then be ready to use the fingers of your left hand.

FINGER EXERCISES ON 'D' STRING

1 Say the rhythm names   **2** Clap the time   **3** Sing the tune   **4** Check hand position *(photographs 4, 5, 6, 7 and 8)*

5 Play very slowly in banjo position and immediately correct any note out of tune before going on to the next one.

Many of the following exercises and pieces have both pizzicato and bowing markings. This is so they can be practised either way – but bowing markings should first be ignored until Step 10 *(see page 16)*. The perfomance tracks on the CD are all played pizzicato until track 16.

UNDER CHIN POSITION
From banjo to under chin

Affix shoulder rest. Hold violin in banjo position, fingers on string. Stand with feet apart and take hold of violin with right hand.

Place violin on shoulder, chin on chin rest, and head a little to left side. Bring left elbow forward without twisting body, or lifting shoulder.

Back view of head and shoulder, with shoulder rest in position. Notice the straight line from knuckles towards elbow.

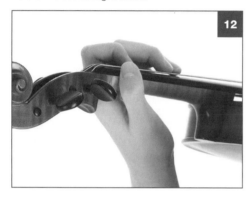

Position of thumb opposite 1st finger.

Top of fingerboard against third crease of 1st finger and fingers bent over the string ready to play.

Standing position with feet apart. Violin held well up with fingers opposite mouth. Right thumb under fingerboard and 1st finger free to pluck.

Practise this position for a few minutes everyday, but do not play in this position until you feel comfortable and secure.

FINGER EXERCISES ON 'D' STRING

Play very slowly in banjo position.

Preliminary exercise to No.5

5 ♩=42 N.B. Both exercises are on track 5 of the CD. No repeat on CD.

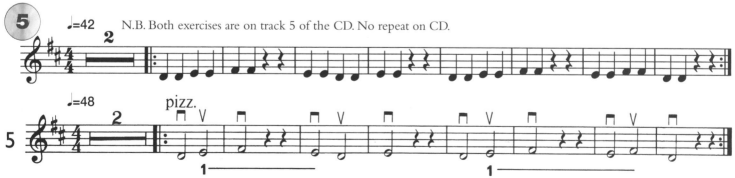

♩=48 pizz.

Now play exercises 3, 4 and 5 pizzicato under your chin – but only if your position is quite correct. Try to play these from memory.

FURTHER FINGER EXERCISES ON 'D' STRING

Banjo position then pizzicato under chin

Practise in the same way as Exercises 3, 4 and 5 – say, clap, sing then play – always slowly, correcting any out-of-tune notes immediately.

Although these pieces are written in minims they could be played as two crotchets to each minim as a preliminary exercise (see No. 5).

From here a minim rest ▬ will replace the two crotchet rests 𝄽 𝄽

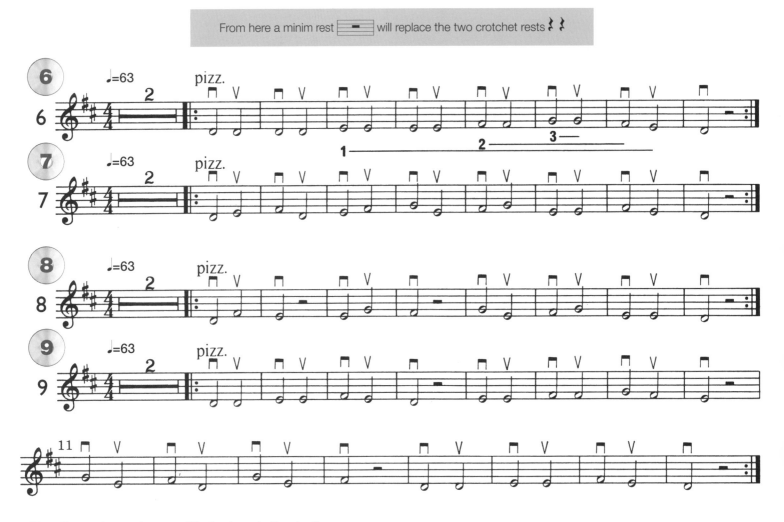

Keep fingers down where possible (as shown in Exercise 6).

Tune the A string in the same way as the D, turning the A string peg or adjuster with the right hand, holding the violin with the left hand and plucking the string with the left thumb.

RHYTHM EXERCISE ON 'D' AND 'A' STRINGS

Say, clap then play. No repeat on CD.

11 FINGER EXERCISE

H = half bow	Pt = point	WB = whole bow

Banjo position then pizzicato under chin

No repeat on CD

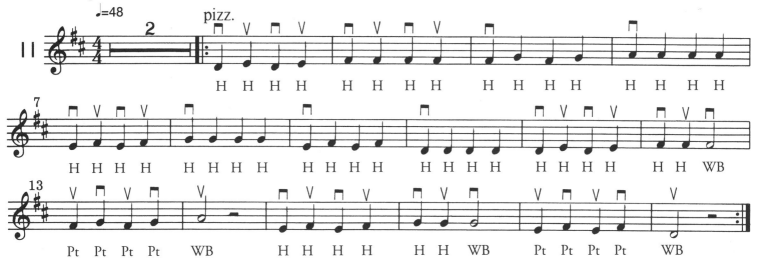

12 THE BELLS OF VENDOME

French Song

No repeat on CD

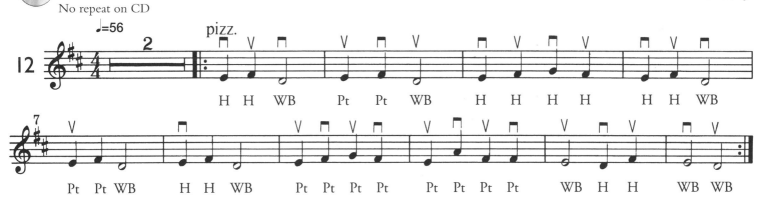

13 NOW THE DAY IS OVER

S. Baring-Gould 1834–1924

No repeat on CD

14 BELLS

Be sure that the 3rd finger is in tune in bar 3, and that in the following bars it falls in *exactly* the same place. It must be placed on the string independently of the other two fingers. When descending take care that the 2nd finger is placed close to the 3rd. This must be done before the 3rd finger is raised.

No repeat on CD

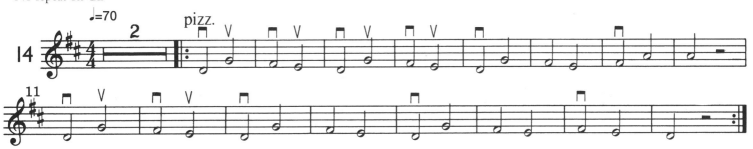

15 HASLEMERE

No repeat on CD

Anonymous

Revise Exercises 8 and 9 under chin. Try to play all pieces from memory when you revise them.

THE BOW-HOLD

Preparation for bow-hold

A Take hold of middle of stick with the left hand, hair facing you, point of bow on your left.

B Raise right arm to shoulder level, upper and forearm at same height. Keep wrist relaxed.

C Place right thumb (slightly bent) on nut at point where it joins stick and forms a ridge. Keep arm in position.

D Place 2nd finger opposite thumb, stick resting on first crease.

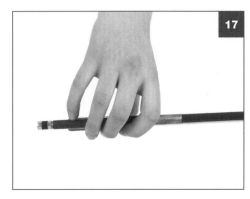

E Bend wrist towards point of bow and the other fingers will fall into position.

F Place 3rd finger almost touching 2nd. Stick should touch fleshy part just above first crease.

G Tip of little finger rests on stick, apart from 3rd finger.

H Place 1st finger apart from 2nd, stick resting between first and second creases and finger curving slightly round stick.

I Let go with left hand. Take care not to grip bow stiffly but hold it firmly. Compare this with photograph 15 and notice how the natural position of the hand stays practically the same when holding the bow.

Now turn your bow over and see if your thumb position is correct.

Practise the bow-hold every day until you can hold the bow with ease.

BOWING SILENTLY

First check bow-hold, then practise through a ring formed by 1st finger and thumb of left hand *(photographs 20 and 21)*. Mark middle of bow with chalk and practise from middle to point only.

Move mainly from elbow, keeping shoulder free and wrist flexible.

Position of arm at middle of bow

Note upward curve of wrist.

Position of arm at point of bow

Note flattened position of wrist.

16 TWINKLE, TWINKLE LITTLE STAR

Traditional Nursery Rhyme

No repeat on CD

17 BLOWING BUBBLES

Polish Folk Song

No repeat on CD

BOWING ON THE 'D' STRING

First check bow-hold, then violin position. Keep right arm at shoulder level and draw bow across D string from middle to point.

Position of arm when playing at middle of bow

Keep bow parallel to and fairly near the bridge.*

Position of arm when playing at point of bow

Watch your bow and keep it on the same spot of the string as it moves downwards. Keep shoulder relaxed and mobile, but move mainly from elbow, keeping wrist flexible.

18 AU CLAIR DE LA LUNE

French Folk Song

*To make sure you bow is moving correctly ask someone to watch it while you are practising, as it's impossible to check this yourself.

19 BOWING EXERCISES ON THE 'D' STRING

Middle to point N.B. All exercises are on track 19 on the CD.

☐ = down bow

V = up bow

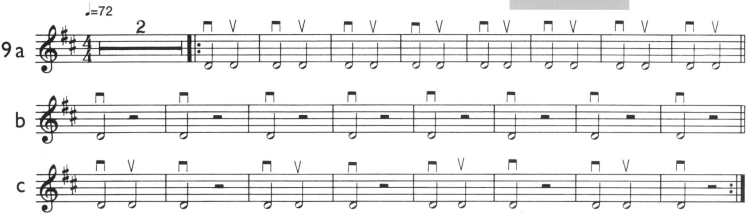

In Exercise 19 (b and c) lift the bow off the string as you count the rests.
Put it on again at the middle of the bow in time to start the following bar.

20 SCALE OF D MAJOR

No repeat on CD

22 ROUSSEAU'S DREAM

J.J. Rousseau *Le Devin du village* 1752

No repeat on CD

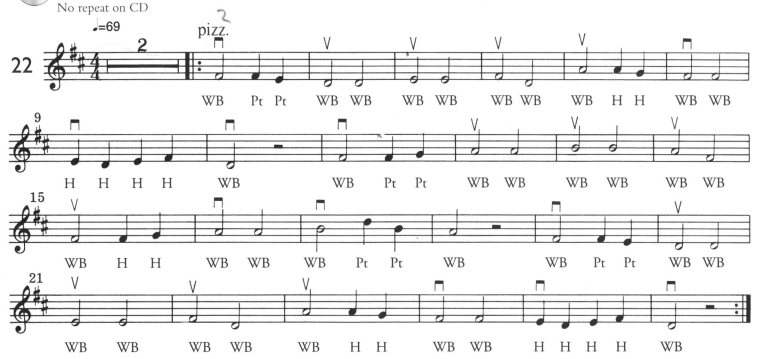

BOWING

Revise Exercises 4 and 5 with the bow. Play very slowly, still bowing only from middle to point. Play from memory and watch your bow to see that it always covers the same spot on the string, fairly near the bridge.

If you prefer to play with quicker bows try Nos. 6-9 but bowing two crotchets for every minim.

At the same time, listen carefully and adjust your finger immediately, even if only *slightly* out of tune. (When using the bow the finger can usually be altered before finishing the note. When playing pizzicato you always had to *repeat* the note.)

Play Exercises 23, 24 and 25 pizzicato under chin without playing them first in banjo position. Play with bow after studying Exercise 40.

23 THERE IS A HAPPY LAND — Indian Air

24 CULBACH — J. Schleffer *Heilge Seelenlust* 1657

25 THE DOVE — Russian Folk Song

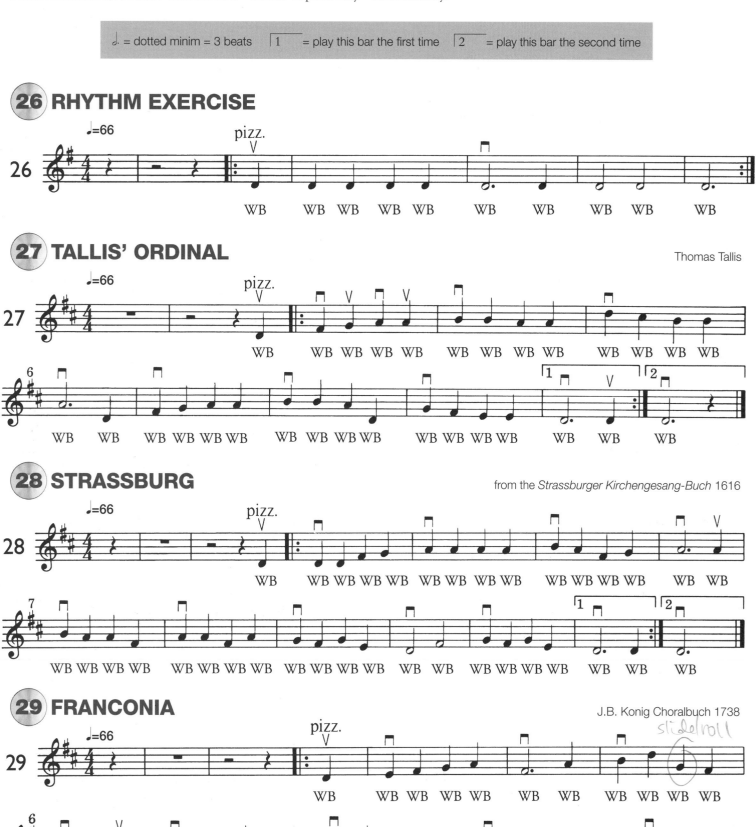

BOWING

Now spend most of your time improving your bowing and spend much less time playing pizzicato.
Practise Exercises 6, 7, 8 and 9 with the bow – middle to point only – from memory.

> 𝅗𝅥. = dotted minim = 3 beats | 1 ‾‾‾ = play this bar the first time | 2 ‾‾‾ = play this bar the second time

26 RHYTHM EXERCISE

27 TALLIS' ORDINAL

Thomas Tallis

28 STRASSBURG

from the *Strassburger Kirchengesang-Buch* 1616

29 FRANCONIA

J.B. Konig Choralbuch 1738

When learning a new piece it is advisable to clap the time and say the rhythm names first, and then play the piece once or twice pizzicato.
Continue to memorise as many pieces as possible.

21

Position of shoulder when playing on 'D' string

Lowered position of shoulder when playing on 'A' string

30 BOWING EXERCISE FOR CHANGING STRINGS

Play from middle to point. When changing from A to D string, lower your arm slightly at shoulder.

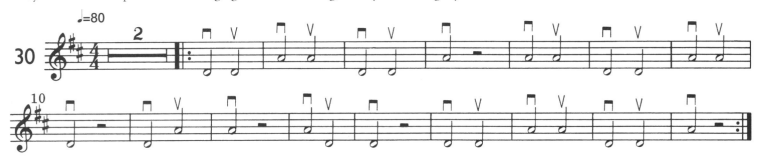

Revise Exercises 14 and 20 (middle to point) from memory (*photographs 22, 23, 24 and 25*).

Position of arm at heel of bow string on 'D' string

Position of arm at middle of bow on 'D' string

Notice that the upper arm changes position when bowing at the heel.

Next practise from heel to middle – this is a whole arm movement. (*See photographs 26 and 27.*)
Revise Exercises 4, 5, 6, 7, 8, 9, 14, 19, 20 and 30. Play them all from heel to middle (you can still practise them from middle to point as well).

H = heel	Pt = point	M = middle	WB = whole bow

You are now ready to join the two half bows, in order to play one note with a whole bow. This is best done in easy stages as in the next two exercises.

The bow rests silently on the string during the rests – but keep the wrist flexible.

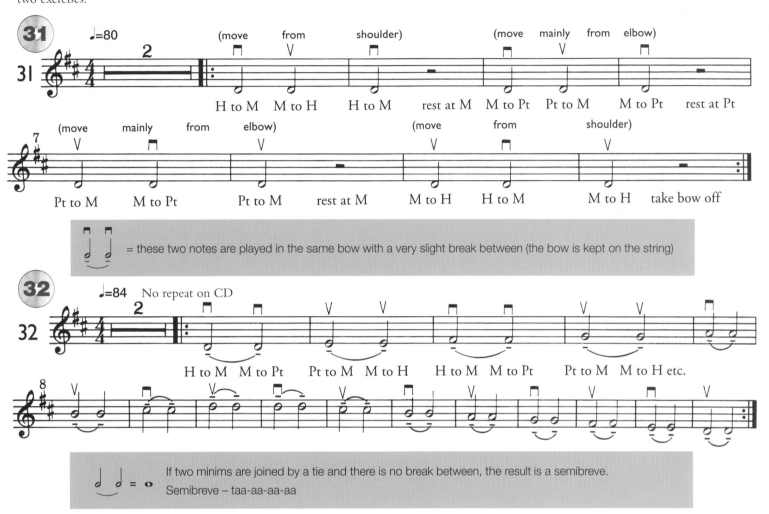

= these two notes are played in the same bow with a very slight break between (the bow is kept on the string)

If two minims are joined by a tie and there is no break between, the result is a semibreve.
Semibreve – taa-aa-aa-aa

33 SCALE OF D MAJOR

Practise slowly at first and gradually speed up the bow. Use WBs for every note.

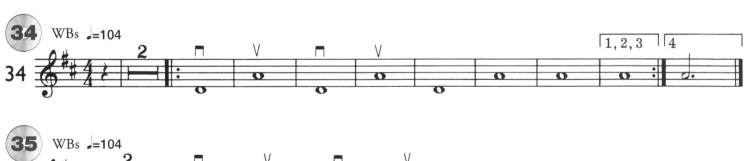

EXERCISES FOR WHOLE BOWS

34 WBs ♩=104

35 WBs ♩=104

When you have practised Step 14 a good deal you will find that your bow gradually starts to move more quickly. Do not force the speed of your bow, but if you can, move it easily from heel to point at a fairly quick pace, trying to use WBs for minims. Lift the bow during the rests and take care when placing it on the string.

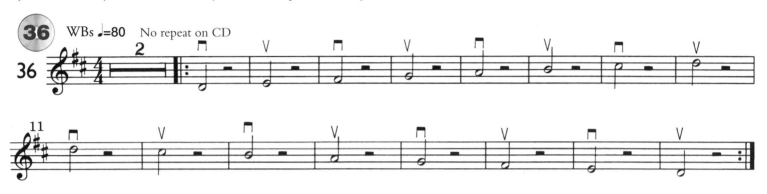

Revise 6, 7, 8, 9, 14 and 20 with whole bows, and also learn the following pieces.

37 A GENTLE BREEZE

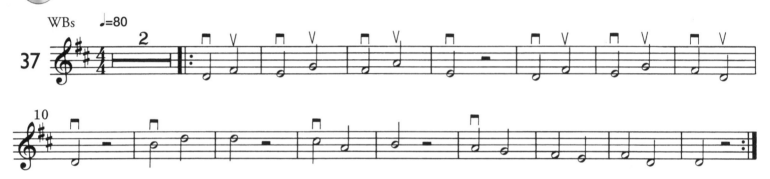

38 DOWN THE STEPS

> ʼ = start of a new phrase; stop the bow for a split second

39 ON THE SWING

40 BOWING EXERCISES USING WHOLE BOWS AND HALF BOWS

Use whole bows (WBs) for minims, half bows (HBs) at either heel (H) or point (pt) for crotchets.

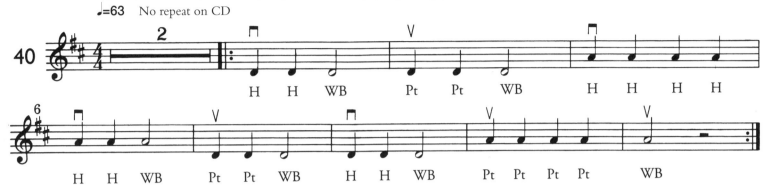

Revise Exercises 11, 12, 13, 15, 16, 17, 18 and 21–25 with the bow. Play with the same bowing as Exercise 40.

This stage is important as you are gaining confidence with the bow, so linger here and make sure you have thoroughly covered all the ground so far.

Now you should be ready to use WBs for crotchets. Continue with the following pieces using WBs for every note, varying the speed: i.e. quick for WBs for crotchets, slow WBs for minims, and slower WBs for dotted minims.

41 CRADLE SONG

German Folk Song

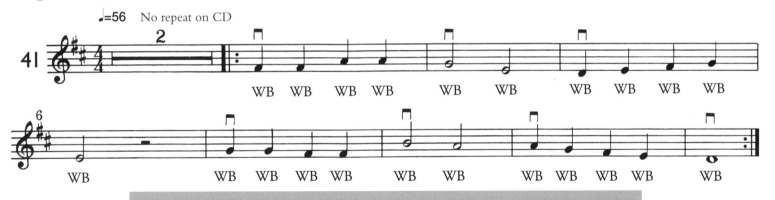

In the following pieces there are only three crotchets in a bar, shown by the time signature **3⁄4**

42 QUEEN MARY

Scottish Folk Song

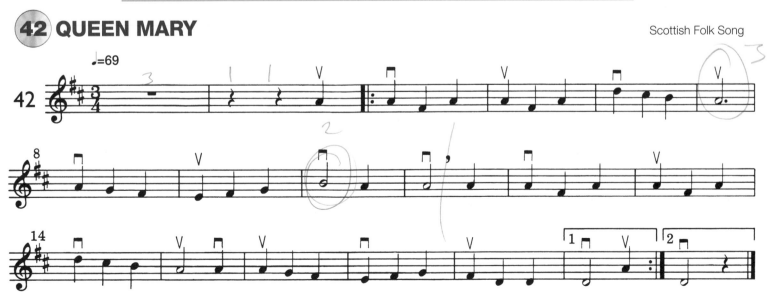

Revise Exercises 27, 28 and 29 using WBs for every note.

Use WBs for crotchets, slower WBs for minims and short bows at each end for quavers.

CD 2&4

1 **RHYTHM EXERCISE**

43 ♩=69

WB WB H H WB   Pt Pt Pt Pt WB   WB WB H H WB   Pt Pt WB WB

2 **MELODY**

44 ♩=69

3 **VILIKINS AND HIS DINAH**

English Song

45 ♩=76

4 **THIS OLD MAN**

English Folk Song

46 ♩=76   No repeat on CD

When you play this piece more quickly, it will not always be necessary to use WBs for the crotchets. Generally, the amount of bow used depends on the speed and character of the music.

As you become more experienced, you will learn to decide for yourself how much bow to use in each piece.

THE 'E' STRING

First, tune the E string as you tuned the A string. When changing from the A to the E string lower your arm slightly at the shoulder.

$\boldsymbol{p}$ = piano-soft	= crescendo – getting gradually louder
$\boldsymbol{f}$ = forte – loud	= diminuendo – getting gradually softer

5 FRÈRE JACQUES

French Folk Song

6 MERRY MAY

$\frac{2}{4}$ = 2 beats in a bar

German Folk Song

7 MAY DAY

German Song

mf = fairly loud   mp = fairly soft   pp = very soft

8 SCALE OF A MAJOR

♩=60   No repeat on CD

9 THE BILLY GOAT

Russian Folk Song

♩=72   No repeat on CD

10 LITTLE BROWN JUG

R.A. Eastburn

♩=108   No repeat on CD

11 GERMAN FOLK SONG

♪ ╕ = quaver and quaver rest

♩=80

If you can play Exercise 53 at a fairly quick speed, use only the middle of the bow.

Ask about slurs

⌒ = a slur – play all notes connected by a slur in one bow

12 ♩=60 No repeat on CD

54

13 THE VICAR OF BRAY

English Song 17th century

♩=84

55

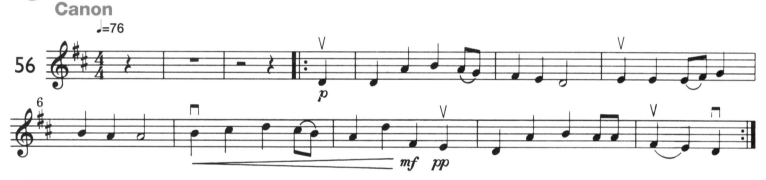

14 ENGLISH FOLK SONG

Canon

♩=76

56

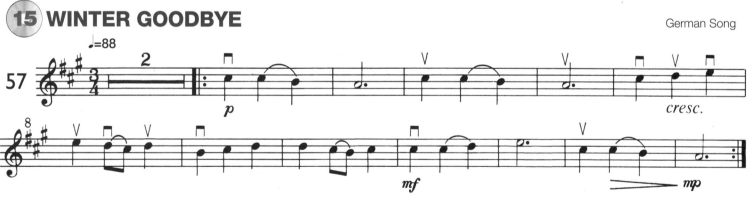

15 WINTER GOODBYE

German Song

♩=88

57

16 4TH FINGER EXERCISE*

4 = 4th finger

♩=60

58

*Note to the teacher: it is a little early to teach 4th finger, but this exercise might help to set the hand in the correct position if the pupil is having difficulty. Much depends on the size of the hand and the flexibility of the fingers. If the 4th finger is bought in at this stage, the fingering can be added to some of the following pieces. For further examples in use of 4th finger see Book 2.

17 WALTZ

Start in the middle of the bow

♩=92 No repeat on CD

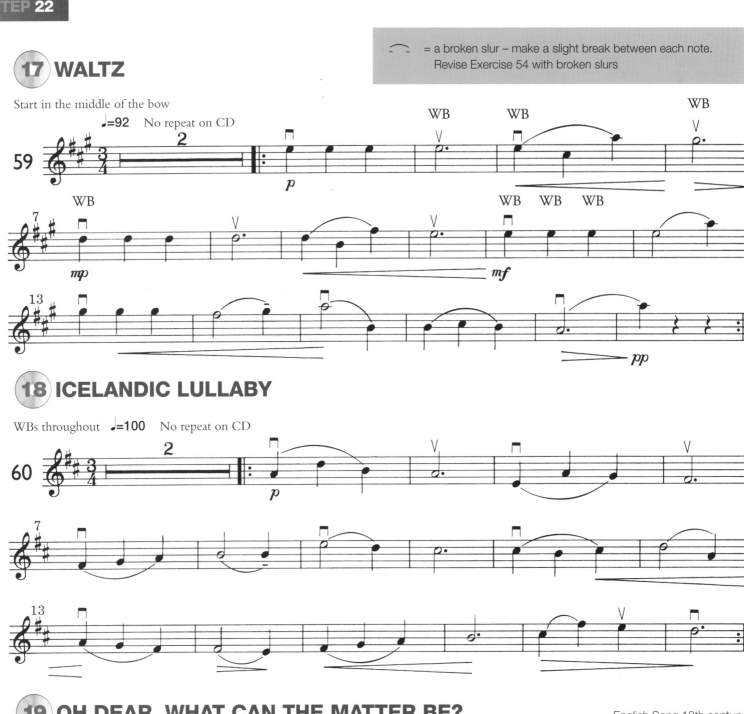

18 ICELANDIC LULLABY

WBs throughout ♩=100 No repeat on CD

19 OH DEAR, WHAT CAN THE MATTER BE?

English Song 18th century

WBs throughout ♩=92 No repeat on CD

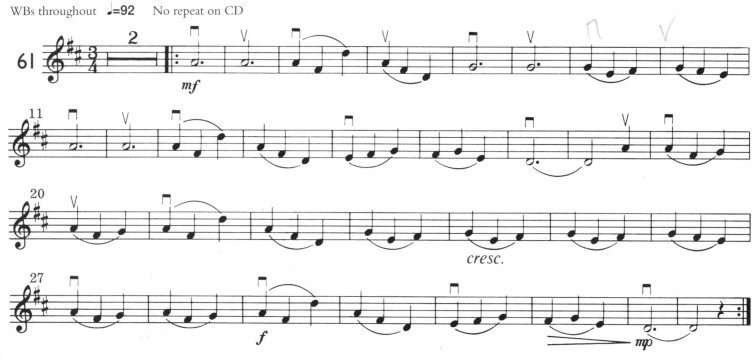

= a broken slur – make a slight break between each note.
Revise Exercise 54 with broken slurs

♩. = dotted crotchet – 1 ½ beats   ♩♪ = taa-aa-tai

23 RHYTHM EXERCISES

Carefully compare a, b and c. N.B. All exercises are on CD track 23.

65a

b

c

24 HERE'S A HEALTH UNTO HIS MAJESTY

English Song 1667

66

25 THE MERRY HAYMAKERS

English Folk Song

67

When playing on the G string the arm should be slightly higher than when you play on the D.

26 SCALE OF G MAJOR

27 KEYS OF HEAVEN

Cheshire Folk Song

28 SWEET ENGLAND

English Folk Song

29 APPROACH OF WINTER

German Folk Song

30 EXERCISE IN DOUBLE STOPPING

arco = with the bow

31 THE FIDDLER

♩=88   No repeat on CD

*Keep your bow in your hand.

32 DRINK TO ME ONLY

English Song

♩=92   No repeat on CD

Here is a very useful piece for practising at the heel of the bow. This is always a difficult part of the bow as the tone tends to be scratchy. Hold the bow firmly but do not press.

Make sure that the little finger is in position and keep all the fingers flexible. Lift the bow off the string for every rest. Use only about 5–6 cms of bow and practise repeatedly until the tone sounds smooth.

33 THE MAN

German Folk Song

♩=72   No repeat on CD

34 PETER PIPER

Traditional Nursery Rhyme

This piece can be practised at the point and then at the middle of the bow.

35 IN THE FOREST

German Folk Song

36 THE HIGHLAND LAD

Scottish Folk Song

37 SUSAN

German Folk Song

♩=92 No repeat on CD

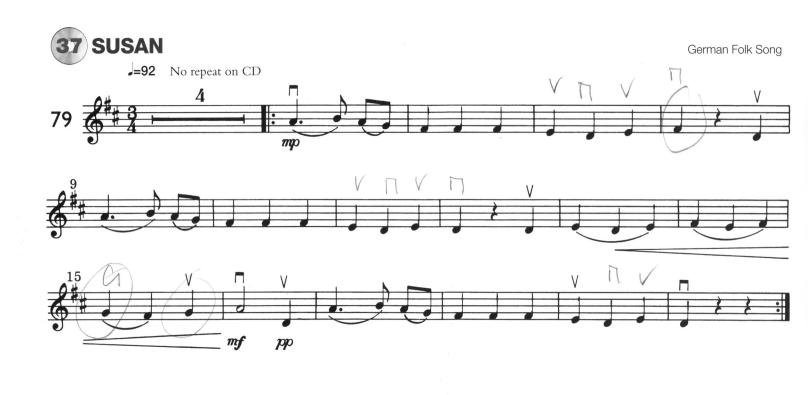

38 THE BIRDS ARE HERE

German Folk Song

♩=96 No repeat on CD

39 DABBLING IN THE DEW

English Folk Song

♩=72 No repeat on CD

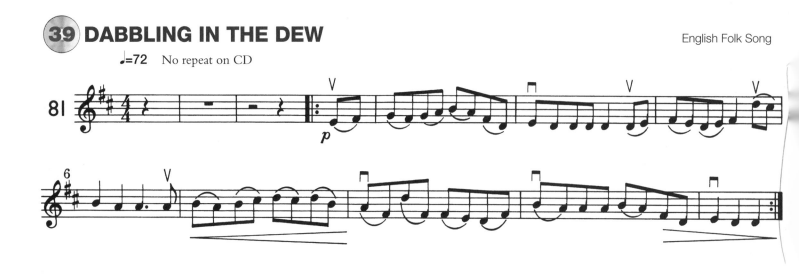

If the pupil finds the pieces on these last two pages rather difficult, they can be studied together with the first part of Book 2, or the pupil can learn them at a later date.

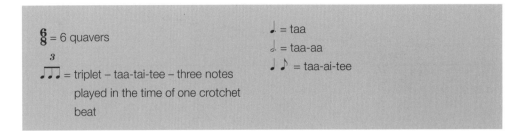

43 RHYTHM EXERCISES

45 LITTLE BO-PEEP

Traditional Nursery Rhyme

46 LAD O'THE NORTH

English Country Dance

1 2 3 4 5 6 7 8 9